The Little Witch & Wizard

Poems by Alethea Kontis
Illustrations by Bianca Roman-Stumpff

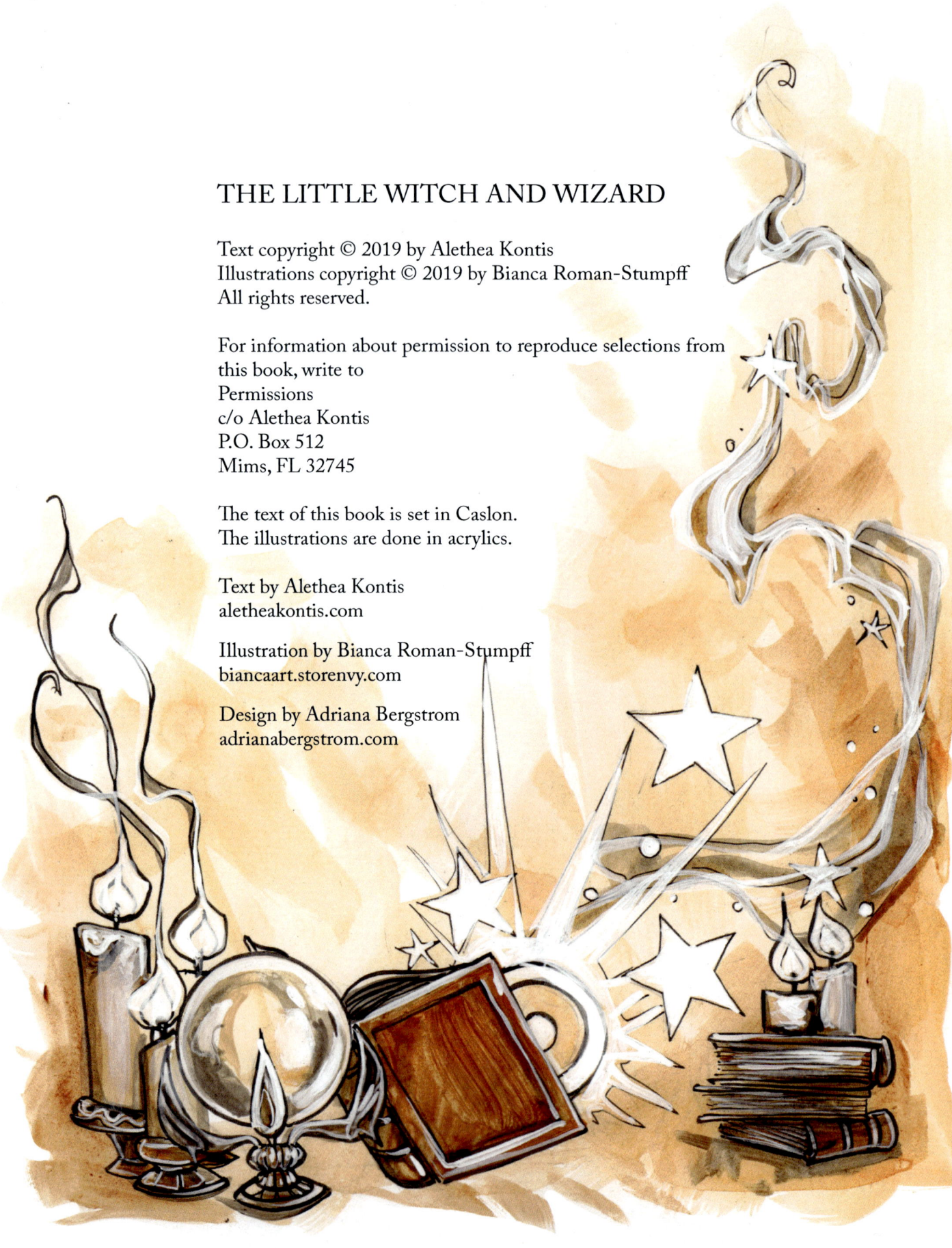

THE LITTLE WITCH AND WIZARD

Text copyright © 2019 by Alethea Kontis
Illustrations copyright © 2019 by Bianca Roman-Stumpff
All rights reserved.

For information about permission to reproduce selections from this book, write to
Permissions
c/o Alethea Kontis
P.O. Box 512
Mims, FL 32745

The text of this book is set in Caslon.
The illustrations are done in acrylics.

Text by Alethea Kontis
aletheakontis.com

Illustration by Bianca Roman-Stumpff
biancaart.storenvy.com

Design by Adriana Bergstrom
adrianabergstrom.com

For Justine and Maureen,
who are made of magic.

To Do List

Grab your books, a rag, a broom,
Do your homework, clean your room
Make your bed and sweep the floor,
Put away your laundry…

OR

Gather eyeballs in a jar
Conjure sky and catch a star
Make a mudpie, make a friend
Build a fort and play pretend

Squeeze in all the tasks that fit
This day's what you make of it!

Recipe for Happiness

Add these things to your witch's brew
Two drops of dusk and morning dew
Three twinkles from a starry sky
Four kisses from a butterfly
One silver apple, cut in half
One beldam's smile, one baby's laugh
Verbena and gold root for spice
Six rose petals, then stir it thrice

A tincture of this happy stew
Will help you when you're feeling blue!

Teamwork

Our interests and talents
Are quite different but
We're mighty together
And no matter what

In passion and power
We two are well paired
And we know that magic
Is better when shared

From sunbeams to starshine
From midnight to noon
Let's challenge each other
Let's shoot for the moon

Learning to Fly

Sometimes I just want to fly
Feel the wind and touch the sky
Climb and swoop and glide and zoom
Sweep the sky upon a broom
Leave all cares and fears behind
Fill my heart and clear my mind
Let myself be blown away
Trust the lamp to light my way

I wish that and so much more
I hold tight
And hope
And soar.

Mishap

While studying one must confess
Experiments make such a mess
To wish for luck would be remiss
There is no luck involved in this
There is no where or when or why
The only way is just to try
Fail once, fail twice, then fail again
Count up to five, then count to ten
When you're face down upon the floor
Get right back up and try once more
For every chance we take we earn
And messing up is how we learn

Conjuring the Deep

Sailors bold and pirate knaves
Tell of beasts among the waves
Kraken's ink and narwhal's tooth
Siren's call and turtle's truth

No adventure is complete
Without monsters to defeat
Gather courage, shed no tear
Cast your spell and face your fear

But be sure you know your foe
Not all beasts bring shock and woe
Keep in mind that in the end
You might make that fiend your friend!

Books Are An Adventure

Books are an adventure
A journey that we take
A dream of lands both near and far
While we are still awake

Books are a connection
To treasured tales that sing
Of hope, adventure, love and loss
They cover everything

Books are a collection
A lettered lost and found
With each new word and phrase and thought
Our minds can soar unbound!

Good Enough

We sweated and struggled
We troubled and toiled
We tossed all the items
That ended up spoiled

We pushed and persisted
No matter the cost
When even our patience
Was something we'd lost

We started out wide-eyed
Just gems in the rough
Till practice makes perfect
We'll take good enough!

You Are Cordially Invited

Please join us on
This lovely day
It's time for tea
And time to play

Come one, come all
Come low, come high
Come large, come small
Come far, come nigh

The fun starts here
And never ends
So let's take tea
And make new friends

Friendship

It's hard to mend
A broken heart
When two dear friends
Are far apart

To keep in touch
With those you've met
Reach out, catch up
Never forget

In times of grief
And darkest night
True friendship brings
Us love and light

Divination

No fortune told is set in stone
The future you make is your own
No matter what the cards construe
My destiny is here with you
Whatever our fates have in store
I'll be your friend forevermore!

Ghost Stories

Some tales tell of romance
And fortune and fame
Some tales are fantastic
But end just the same

But some tales are told with
A whisper and moan
And dastardly devils
Of shadows and bone

They tie you in tangles
Trap you in a maze
And leave you with nightmares
That haunt you for days

When you want a story
A ghost would endorse
Remember the best tales
Come straight from the source!

Made in the USA
Middletown, DE
07 September 2019